P9-CFF-763

It's about Time

Hours

by Kimberly M. Hutmacher

Gail Saunders-Smith, PhD,
Consulting Editor

CAPSTONE PRESS
a capstone imprint

Pebble Books are published by Capstone Press,
1710 Roe Crest Drive, North Mankato, Minnesota 56003
www.capstonepub.com

Library of Congress Cataloging-in-Publication Data
Hutmacher, Kimberly
  Hours / by Kimberly M. Hutmacher.
     p. cm.—(Pebble Books. It's about time)
  Includes bibliographical references and index.
  Summary: "Simple rhyming text and color photographs present hours as a unit of
time"—Provided by publisher.
  ISBN 978-1-4296-8577-1 (library binding)
  ISBN 978-1-4296-9350-9 (paperback)
  ISBN 978-1-62065-283-1 (ebook PDF)
  1. Time—Juvenile literature. 2. Time measurements—Juvenile literature. 3. Clocks
and watches—Juvenile literature. I. Title.
  QB209.5.H884 2013
  529'.2—dc23   2012004668

Note to Parents and Teachers

The It's about Time set supports national mathematics
standards related to measurement and data. This book describes
and illustrates hours. The images support early readers in
understanding the text. The repetition of words and phrases helps
early readers learn new words. This book also introduces early
readers to subject-specific vocabulary words, which are defined
in the Glossary section. Early readers may need assistance to read
some words and to use the Table of Contents, Glossary, Read More,
Internet Sites, and Index sections of the book.

Printed in the United States of America in North Mankato, Minnesota.
042012   006682CGF12

Table of Contents

What Is an Hour?

An hour is
a chunk of time.
To see how long,
let's read this rhyme!

one hour

minute hand

hour hand

second hand

Telling Time with Hours

Tick, tock, analog clock.

We measure time on its face.

Second, minute, hour hands—

always keeping pace!

Every 60 minutes
the hour hand creeps ...
slowly to the next big number,
putting you to sleep.

hours   colon

Bright lights of digital clocks
measure minutes and hours.
The hour's first, before the colon.
The hour has the power!

12

How Long Is an Hour?

An hour passes by you when ...

You write a story.

Play one-on-one.

Build a castle.

Fun! Fun! Fun!

14

Paint a picture.

Grocery shop.

Take a dance class.

Hip! Hip! Hop!

Watch a show.

Dust and sweep.

Pile leaves.

Leap! Leap! Leap!

20

That's an hour.
Time sure flies!
Sixty minutes—
ticking by!

Glossary

analog clock—a clock with minute and hour hands and usually a second hand

clock—a machine used to measure and show time

digital clock—a clock that displays hours and minutes separated by a colon; digital clocks do not have hands

face—the front side of a clock; it shows the numbers and hands of the clock

hand—a pointer on a clock

hour—a measure of time equal to 60 minutes

pace—a rate of speed

Read More

Karapetkova, Holly. *Seconds, Minutes, and Hours.* Concepts. Vero Beach, Fla.: Rourke Pub., 2010.

Rosa-Mendoza, Gladys. *What Time Is It?* My World. New York: Windmill Books, 2011.

Steffora, Tracey. *Clocks and Calendars.* Measuring Time. Chicago: Heinemann Library, 2011.

Internet Sites

FactHound offers a safe, fun way to find Internet sites related to this book. All of the sites on FactHound have been researched by our staff.

Here's all you do:

Visit *www.facthound.com*

Type in this code: 9781429685771

Check out projects, games and lots more at
www.capstonekids.com

Index

Word Count: 134
Grade: 1
Early-Intervention Level: 16

Editorial Credits
Gillia Olson, editor; Lori Bye, designer; Sarah Schuette, photo stylist;
   Marcy Morin, studio scheduler; Kathy McColley, production specialist

Photo Credits
All photos by Capstone Studio/Karon Dubke except:
   iStockphoto/DNY59, 20